Preacher's Daughter Anthology:

Poetry, Prayers, Joys and Lamentations

By

Jennifer Casandra Williams Herring, PhD

And some submissions by Glen Etta Williams

Me(1972) and Glen (1967)

MMBA Press
Springfield   Dallas

Preacher's Daughter Anthology: Poetry, Prayers, Joys and Lamentations. Copyright © 2011 by Jennifer Casandra Williams Herring, PhD and Glen Etta Williams, First Edition. All rights reserved. Printed in the United States of America. No part of this book may be reproduced in whole or in part, in any form, without the express written authorization of Jennifer Casandra Williams Herring, PhD.

ISBN: 978-0-9746843-4-5

Contents

Dedication	v
Preface	vii
Acknowledgements	x
So to Speak	1
God, did you really give me this assignment?	2
Surrender	3
On Being 51	4
The Way of the Snail	9
Right Outside My Window	10
Keep the Faith	11
Thank you Holy Spirit	12
The Apocalypse	13
Homeward, Upward	15
Thoughts and Directions	16
I Will See You	17
Kindness Peace and Mercy Shall	18
Thaw	19
Poem 1 – Thy Word	21
Poem 2 – A Vow	22
Poem 3 – Put A Message in my Mouth	23
Poem 4 – Do not be Afraid	25
Poem 5 – A Treasured Possession	26
Poem 6 – Create in Me	27
Poem 8 – Have Mercy on Me	28
Poem 9 – Today I Am	29
Poem 10 – Father I Have Sinned	30

Poem 13 – Come Unto Me	31
Poem 14 – Judges 7	33
Poem 15 – Making A Vow	34
Poem 16 – Teach Me, Master	35
Poem 17 – The Doors	36
Poem 18 – The Mockery of A King	37
Poem 19 – Death Comes A Little Closer	38
Poem 20 – Fight No More	39
Photograph Credits	40

This anthology is dedicated in love to those who love the Lord and abide by His calling, who have failings, but know of the redemptive power of God's love.

To understand others is to understand yourself (Author Unknown).

Preface

Life presents itself in ebbs and flows I have learned. What happens during the ebbs affect what happens during the flows and all of life's in-betweens. Handling all of this as a preacher's daughter presents a different outlook, a different call to purpose, a different challenge to the dips and curves. My sister Glen Etta is ten years or so older than me. She presents herself in the light of a woman with a passion that has extinguished itself slowly over time and only feels the fire when one mentions the name of Jesus. Jesus is her husband, Jesus is her Rock, and just Jesus is her Friend. As a matter of fact, Glen says Jesus is returning the Summer of 2011. It matters not that she re-adjusts this announcement every year. Glen Etta is retired: tired from the ebbs and flows, tired from seeing the same people doing the same things, herself included. So she waits. Her writings, poetry in this text indicate just that: *Thank You Holy Spirit*, *Keep the Faith*, *The Apocalypse*, *Thaw*, *Homeward-Upward*, *Thoughts and Directions*, *I Will See You,* and *Kindness Peace and Mercy, Shall* all point to the soon coming of the King, King Jesus. I had to cajole and challenge her to share these writings, but I wanted to put them down, share them with the world. It is from such sharing that we understand the mind of each other, that we understand the connections to upbringing and our future and later years in life. How the drenching of the Holy Scriptures affect us, going forward: sometimes positively, sometimes uniquely, but most times directing our goings and comings, our 'fixin-to', 'have-to' and 'got-to' do something in order to make sense of this world and the world to come. Glen Etta reads the Holy Scriptures every day, religiously. She has her own private conversations with 'Jesus', her man, every day, and even while you might be talking to her on the phone. It does not harm anyone when she does so, as so many of us have quirks just as far-reaching: talking and texting; driving, talking and texting; talking on the phone while walking, yelling out to others, while talking on the phone. 21st Century skill some would say, but still quite quirky.

On the other hand, I am very quietly marking my big sister's footsteps, being careful not to follow exactly, but be alongside her now. I too love to communicate, especially the written word. I love to read it and I love to write it. As a preacher's daughter as well, I carry the history of ingesting lots of text, lots of Holy Scripture, lots of passion for living. Out of my belly flows 'rivers of living water' so spoken of by Jesus Christ himself in the King James Version of the Holy Bible in the book of St. John, Chapter 7, verse 38: *He that believeth on me as the scripture has said, out of his belly shall flow rivers of living water.* And yes, I believe on Him, Jesus Christ, as the scripture has said. In this book are writings, lamentations, prayer and poetry that have flowed out. Poems that form my lips in prayer some days like *Father I Have Sinned* and *Judges 7*. It continues to flow every day, regardless of my current circumstances, current place in this life.

When it stops flowing, I will stop existing. I know that now.

My musings are a bit different from my big sister Glen Etta's musings, yet we both were raised in the same family under the same Daddy-preacher, Elder John Morgan Williams, Sr. Glen Etta is more spiritual, more scriptural in her approach. I on the other hand am concrete-woman. I take what I know of the Holy Scriptures and translate it through my life, my real life happenings – my poetry speaks to my situations, like *The Way of the Snail*. These approaches are reflected throughout the book. They are prayers, thoughts from our hearts to yours. We are the daughters that sat quietly, learned quietly. We live quietly. But the soul is on fire, always. Always singing, always wondering, always believing, trusting in His Holy Word. He never failed us yet.

ACKNOWLEDGEMENTS

This book is dedicated in loving memory of my dear Father, the Preacher, Elder John Morgan Williams Sr., my dear middle sister, Brenda Ann Williams and my dear oldest brother, Earl Lee Williams.

Jennifer C. Herring
February 2011

So, to Speak

Life's Intersections – A Wordle

Breech-blue-eyes-brown-eyes-pneumonia-alive-smart-talker-quiet-reflective-calm-spiffy-Mrs. Simmons-egghead-goat-head-short plaits-skinny legs-peppermint-Miss Librarian-Bethune-Maypole-girl-nerd-drown-fighter-sanctified-peacemaker-Cathy-books-Bobbsey Twins-Nancy Drew-Spanish Club-Northeast High-VP-Dallas-computers-projects-tambourine-NHS-Bishop-Deerfield-Brenda-Nate-Christian-maverick-couple-graduate-Roy-programmer-Daddy-Holy Ghost-Singleton-Glen-faimont-faith-Jesse-drums-masters-detention-Deangela-judge-Spence-Contreras-Black-adoption-teacher-chrch-specialist-cruise-Catholic-fibroids-Carlos-sing-Africa-Trenishia-Mother-suburbs-Yale-downsized-pool-Laurenzo-PhD-scouts-culture-35e-books-PDA-Sawgrass-mom-reunion-Cherry-train-Capitol-3rd-Foundations-Teacher Education-UIS-AFCC-weight-tenure-Lanphier-troop 2607-Anderson-WWA-undergraduate council—China-NAME-Calvary-police-no tenure—SJR-Michael-health-YMCA-sing-UBC and so, to speak.

Jennifer Casandra Williams Herring

God, did you really give me this assignment?

I used *confluent* in writing a draft of my two-year personnel review just recently. The report was due on Monday, January 23, 2006. I used this word in an introduction paragraph of the review, referring to how my life as a newly hired tenure-track professor at the University of Illinois at Springfield has been one that challenges me to absorb, learn, prepare, teach, read, write and serve *confluently* as expected. Every working moment, I have been inhaling and exhaling what I *should* be doing versus what I *am* doing precariously measuring the two against each other. Alongside this I am trying to keep family and friends in view, at last on my email list.

My work as a professor demands that I lead a lifestyle that incorporates all that I am and do. For me, it is not about leaving the job at the job and moving on to the next activity at home and with friends. I have to bring the family to the workplace and the workplace goes home with me most times. Gratefully, I have been able to do both. Making sure the family is on campus at various times, involved like playing the jembe drums in the UIS percussion group, singing in the UIS Chorus, catching some of the UIS theatre performances.

One of the requirements of the professorate is to do work according to Boyer's method: spending time teaching, doing scholarly activities and community service. How do you do all of these things without burning out so quickly? Perhaps working smarter and not harder would mean I allow what I do to count in more than one category, blending as much as possible. Yeah, that is *confluence*. I have got to be careful though. This word sounds too much like the super-mom syndrome from the 80's, sounds too much like a re-hashed balancing act to me.

After note: I wrote this piece as a writing exercise with the Women's Writer's Association in 2006. Needless to say, at this writing I did not get tenure in this position. After all the work, all the sacrifice, all the tears and perseverance, I was not granted tenure. A valuable lesson was learned. Keep your family and loved ones closer. The will of the Lord be done.

Jennifer Casandra Williams Herring

Surrender

He said you will do what I say, go where I say go…
I said "ok."

He said you were thinking this thought, you said this…
I said "yes."

He said patient! I can't promise you the moon,
I can't promise you anything, not even a life with me…
I said "alright."

Ok, I did it; I said it; I waited…

Jennifer Casandra Williams Herring

On Being 51

It is like never having to take a long time to make a decision

all of what has been learned from the past 50 years of existence

goes into a split second decision.

Never looking back, not longing for what I should have said, what I should have done.

I have all of my hairs on my head,

except now every once in awhile a gray one peeks out

from my otherwise strategically colored nappy tendrils.

I have favorite hair-styles that suit me, fit my many-sided personality.

I care less and less what anyone else has to say about that.

I chuckle a lot, smile more

pitying anyone who wants to rain on my parade.

My breath is reserved for specific, focused use,

mainly those whom I love so dearly,

especially those who love me dearly.

My prayers are more and more for others,

rather than my own selfish desires.

I pray for the expedient health and wellness of my loved ones,

far and near, new and old, known and unknown.

I pray that they enjoy the fleeting simplicities of life,

the God-given earth, sun, moon and stars

and all that dwell therein.

I take care of my God-given children and husband

the best way I know how, with no regrets.

Included in that is taking care of me.

I use the emergency airplane instructions for my well-being.

I put the oxygen mask on my face first,

then I serve my significant others.

I have loved and lost, lost and loved.

I know now that this is one of life's little secrets;

embracing the good, the bad and the ugly.

Being alive to tell the story is a gift.

Speaking of gifts,

I give those rather sparingly now.

I give not to get others to see me, to like me.

I give gifts of what I want, to whom I want, and when I want.

Hopefully, those on the receiving end

know how to graciously accept what is now theirs

with no strings attached, no pretense,

no returns, no "nothing", just an act of love.

I see my Mother in myself,

her womanly weaknesses passed on to me.

Her strength of solitude, quietness and patience

slowly descending upon me like

an early morning dew resting on baby's butt-soft rose petals.

My Daddy's chromosomes are jumbled in the mix.

My progesterone surges with his assurance, passion

and quest to know and tell to any and all who will listen.

I rise up early every morning,

activating his favorite work ethic quote

from the KJV Holy Bible, the Book of Proverbs,

Chapter 6, verses 6, 7 and 8:

"Go to the ant thou sluggard;

consider her ways, and be wise;

which having no guide, overseer or ruler;

provideth her meat in the summer,

and gathereth her food in the harvest."

I am a workaholic by birth and now choice.

I choose to work and I choose what work I want to do.

More than Daddy did however,

I work hard but I play equally as hard.

I ponder the number of days I might have left to live out
the rest of my birthdays.
My feet do not hesitate to walk mornings
around Washington Park,
for every annual doctor's visit reminds me
of how this extends my health less painfully.

Morning coffee has become an old friend.
I moderate its consumption to four-five times
a week, one cup.
That's just in case the research bears true
that coffee is indeed more harmful than delicious
to my health.

I am returning to my spiritual self,
allowing her to manifest me in the existence of the abstract,
the untouchables, the Holy Ghost,
the Word of the Lord.
I desire to explore, accept what I have squelched
concerning those things I cannot see, feel, touch, hear or smell,
with no judgment, no opinion.

Absolutely, I understand now that the more I know only shows up the more that I do not know.

My knowledge, awareness is just a mere drop in the bottomless bucket of God's infinite wisdom, knowledge and understanding.
This truly is my Father God's world, year unnumbered for Him, year 51 for me.

Jennifer Casandra Williams Herring

The Way of the Snail

The wheels on the bus go round and round

life does that to you

back to ground zero, back to square one.

Hope keeps alive, and does not disappoint.

It has not happened yet, but keep hoping, it will.

Tribulations make the wheels keep turning

round and round they go.

Striving for the best way, the better life.

Jennifer Casandra Williams Herring

Right Outside My Window

Snowflakes accumulate

right outside my window,

the window of my soul.

I open up to receive

the thoughts of pleasure

contrasting with the cold,

stark whiteness of my environment.

Brown, hard trees stand firm

right outside my window,

the window of my soul.

Waiting on me to choose which

one will be selected to provide

the warmth of fire to calm

my frazzled senses, to singe my soul,

I am here, ready to do this,

Comfort me, O God.

Jennifer Casandra Williams Herring

Keep the Faith

Here's one thing
I found is true
If Jesus said it
That's what He'll do.

If in trying you
He changes His mind
You'll find He'll
Change it back in time.

So keep the faith
And keep His truth
He'll do just what
He said He'd do.

I've learned this lesson
I'm learning it still
It's one that leads
You through the door.

Glen Etta Williams

Thank You Holy Spirit

Thank you Holy Spirit
for your guidance, joy and care
because you dwell within us
we're empowered not to err.
You overshadowed Mary
to conceive and bare the Lord
Christ the King who is the life
and Savior of his own.

And now our Heavenly Father
we thank you for your love
You gave your only begotten Son
sent down from heaven above.
That whosoever would only
believe and repent of all their
sins could seek the Lord and
never perish and have
eternal life within.

Glory to the Holy Spirit
Glory to His Word
Glory to His Holy Power
And He IS the Word.
Glen Etta Williams

The Apocalypse

We are in the Apocalypse

And that is the way it is

The timings of good and evil

and all it's unholy ills.

It's the end of time and now

what's only right will shine

like the stars of heaven

righteous forever and ever, all of time.

The servants of the Lord

will be His Holy Crew

His earthly Holy Family,

going up to heaven too.

They will never be without

hope again or ever key defeat.

Victoriously, His Holy saves

and all will be complete.

Earth will be far left behind

from which they will depart

Going up to glory to live forever,

Forever with the Lord.

Glen Etta Williams

Homeward, Upward

Homeward, upward
I'm ready to go when
The Lord says so.
There's so much more
in heaven to do,
Joy unspeakable
And full of glory, too.
There is nothing down
here to stay for, No!
I'm ready to go when
The Lord says so.

Glen Etta Williams

Thoughts and Directions

Speak little now
of being on earth
relative or unnecessarily.

Think up! Emote!
Positively up! Our
thoughts and thinking
must focus on up.

Up in the rapture
not long from now.
Up to the Lord,
Our King and our Father.

Glen Etta Williams

I Will See You

I will see you
In the rapture
hopefully,
if you're going
home to Jesus.

He is coming
to rescue us.
I will see you
in the rapture
hopefully.

Glen Etta Williams

Kindness Peace and Mercy Shall

When the mountains
shall depart and the
hills be removed
the kindness of
the Lord shall
not depart
though when
tossed with a
tempest and not
comforted behold
His covenant of peace
and mercy shall
cover your soul.

Glen Etta Williams

Thaw

Thaw is the way the Holy Spirit says it
speaking of the Return, for those
who are not quite fully aware, the
Return is about to occur. Thaw
says the Holy Spirit for those who
are not so aware. The Return of
Christ is really upon us, far more
than people share. Get ready. Stay
ready. He's ready, too, the Father and
the Son to return to the world to
seal and catch away all those
who are His own. Get ready.

Stay ready for the sudden Return

for the quick return of the Lord in

all the Glory and Power of the Father.

Men will just be stunned. The

earth shall quake, shake and roll and

tremble and so will the heavens

too as it scrolls apart high up in

the sky and the King sits there

on his throne and next we will

see Him coming in the clouds to

take His children home. So get

ready, stay ready, He's ready too, the

Father and the Son…to take His children

home. To Glory. To both the Father and the Son.

Glen Etta Williams

Poem 1: Thy Word

Dear God,
Just as you have said in your Word,
your Holy Word, your righteous Word,
My Word is a lamp unto thy feet
A light unto they path.
Words enlightened cause spirits to
be consumed, but not your Spirit, Lord.
Your Spirit is your Word, your bond
For eons past and eons to come.

Your Word is a promise, a command,
an order to walk in your will, in your way.
Your Word says the steps of a good man
[or woman] are ordered by You.
Order my steps, one by one, Lord
Year by year, day by day, night by night,
Hour by hour, minute by minute, second by second.
The Word of the Lord, thanks be to God.

Jennifer Casandra Williams Herring

Poem 2: A Vow

Dear God,
I will keep myself here with You
where the depth of my soul crieth out,
yet sings softly and tenderly
yearning for mercy and forgiveness
longing for that unquenchable touch.
Insatiable desire is fulfilled here,
in this place.
The Word of the Lord. Thanks be to God.

Jennifer Casandra Williams Herring

Poem 3: Put a Message in My Mouth

Dear God,

Put a message in my mouth:

Of hope when the day stretches long

And the night descends way after ten-thirty.

Early morning brings renewal to the soul.

Put a message in my mouth:

Of chastisement when the body begins to wane

and seems to forget that its parts make the whole.

A Spirit-Word spoken restores its youth.

Put a message in my mouth:

Of understanding when the days are gone by

And recapture is unfruitful and telling.

Reparation is the life-force for now until forever.

Put a message in my mouth:

Of truthfulness when non-disclosure weakens the soul

And fear along with his little brothers are knocking.

May the words of my mouth be accepted by you, Oh Lord.

Put a message in my mouth:

Of joy when all else seems dismal

And drawing the covers over my face does nothing

May your Joy strengthen me.

The Word of the Lord. Thanks be to God.

Jennifer Casandra Williams Herring

Poem 4: Do Not Be Afraid

    Your commands are righteous.
    You said do not be afraid of any man.
    I am not afraid today.
    Your commands guide me and keep me.

    I will lift up my head.
    Lift up my pen.
    Lift up my thoughts to you, Oh God.
    Teach me to listen, to be still, to know.
    Teach me to cast out fear with your love.

    The Word of the Lord. Thanks be to God.

Jennifer Casandra Williams Herring

I will fear no evil

Poem 5: A Treasured Possession

Dear God,
I am treasured by You as all women
and men are today. Thank you for
refining me, polishing me.

I am Your diamond in the rough.
Rough around the edges, severed
by the un-sanctity of life attacks.

You make me feel brand new,

day by day my faith in You
is renewed as I make my
abode in this present life.

I am incapable of love, a soft
heart, unless You caress me with
your mighty power, Your Holy
Ghost from on High.

Jennifer Casandra Williams Herring

Poem 6 – Create in Me

Dear God,
Create in me a clean heart
Renew in me a right Spirit.
Give me the Words to say,
The life to live.
My body aches

My soul longs for love,
A touch, a caress, a stroke
A fuck –
A child.

The Word of the Lord. Thanks be to God.

Jennifer Casandra Williams Herring

Poem 8: Have Mercy on Me

Dear God,
Have mercy on my soul.
Have mercy on my body
Have mercy on me.

Just as you time and time again
In your Word,
Slayed the enemies of Joshua
And slayed the enemies
Of the Israelites,
Slay my enemies.
Those who would seek to devour

My soul for the taking
To use my being
For their own pleasures
Slay them!

You alone are God
You know my thoughts anyway
You know my desires anyway
You know my insides anyway
And outsides anyway.
Have mercy on me!
The Word of the Lord. Thanks be to God.

Jennifer Casandra Williams Herring

Poem 9: Today I am

Dear God,
Today I am –
    Going to lift up my head
    Oh ye hung down child
    Walk in your place of presence.

Today I am –

      Going to chart my progress
      Continue on my path to
      Righteous of life.

Today I am –
      Going to allow the love
      Of God to permeate my
      Soul, body, mind and
      Spirit.

Today I am –
      Going to forget those things
      That are behind and press
      Forward to those things that
      Are ahead.

Today I am –
      Going to ask you to create in me
      A clean heart and right Spirit,
      Oh God.

The Word of the Lord. Thanks be to God.

Jennifer Casandra Williams Herring

======================

Poem 10: Father I have Sinned

Dear God,
Father, I have sinned. How my discipline

is so lacking in the face of adversity.
How I so need thee every hour, oh bless
me now my Savior. I come to thee.

Father, give me the strength to be ever
near you, ever listening to your small,
still voice, telling me to go ahead, that
you understand, that you sent your Son,
Jesus Christ as the eternal propitiation for
me. Just for me and just for others. I
believe on Him and shall not perish, but
have everlasting life. Thank you, Father.

The Word of the Lord. Thanks be to God.

Jennifer Casandra Williams Herring

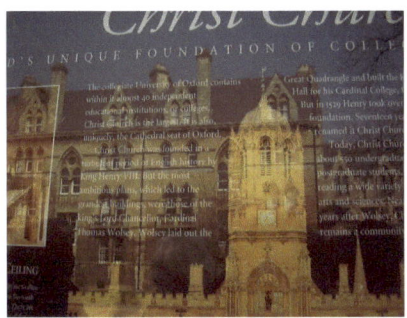

Poem 13: Come Unto Me

Come here and rest
My laurels will cloak you
My strength will stroke you.

Come here to me
now is the time
ten days, no, seven days
of rest.

I will comfort you
in the middle of the night.
I will wake and hold you
my strength will stroke you.

What I have I give
unto you my love
my sweetness,
my strength will stroke you.

Jennifer Casandra Williams Herring

Poem 14: Judges 7

Lapping dogs are the best.

Dogs that lap are the best.
They watch and prey.
They prey and watch.

Never know when enemy #1
is lurking.
Never know when.

God sent an army of lapping dogs
to capture Gideon's enemy.
They watched Gideon.
The preyed their enemy away.

The Word of the Lord. Thanks be to God.

Jennifer Casandra Williams Herring

Poem 15: Making a Vow

Make one
With the purest of intentions.
Ask God, if you need to break it.

Jennifer Casandra Williams Herring

Poem 16: Teach Me, Master

Oh, Teach me Master,
    teach me.
Teach me how to act.
Teach me how to pray, then act.
Teach me how to pray, then act, then wait.
Teach me that when I have done what I
    should do, then to wait and
see what you will do.

The Word of the Lord. Thanks be to God.

Jennifer Casandra Williams Herring

Poem 17: The Doors

The Doors of the house of the Lord
    Are now open
Will you come?
    Come!
Come on in the house.

The Word of the Lord. Thanks be to God.

Jennifer Casandra Williams Herring

Poem 18: The Mockery of a King

Uh huh. Give me a king.

Who will reign over me
over my fruit – the
fruit of my womb, my land, my produce.

I want a king who will use
me as chattel, as feed for his
gain, my loss.

I want a king that takes away,
not giveth, that hords,
not shares.

Oh Israel, you say you want a
king – here it is, laid out
before you, the words as
spoken by Samuel, as spoken
by God.

Yet you still say give me a king
who will take my daughters

and make them kitchen-goddesses,
who will take my sons and make
drivers and workers for you, for

your reign-ship.

Do us and do us good, O king!

The Word of the Lord. Thanks be to God.

Jennifer Casandra Williams Herring

Poem 19: Death Comes a Little Closer

Death comes a little closer
when its late at night
and the clock strikes twelve.
One two, three, four, five,
six, seven, eight, nine, ten,
eleven, then twelve.

When you hear your heart beat
one turn at a time, slowly,
one breath at a time, slowly.
When the night is trestled
with a blinking red pole light
signaling the way for air traffic,
this way to heaven, please.

Jennifer Casandra Williams Herring

Poem 20: Fight No More

Let your soul rest.
Your body be still,
your mind embrace the silence.
Life is silent now.
You can not have it your way,
McDonald's can.
You can be in it, though,
You can be in it.
Present. Here. No more.

Jennifer Casandra Williams Herring

Photograph Credits
All of the photographs are from the scrapbook albums of Jennifer Casandra Williams Herring.

About the Authors:

Jennifer Casandra Williams Herring

At this writing, Dr. Jennifer Casandra Williams Herring is Assistant Professor in the Teacher Education department at the University of Illinois at Springfield, teaching courses such as Technology for Teachers, History and Philosophy of Education and Exceptional Child for Teachers. She also the Director of Technology and e-Learning for Duplichain University. She teaches adjunct for the University of North Texas and Duplichain University, several graduate education courses including Teaching Diverse Populations. She conducts a variety of workshops, with experience in multicultural education, technology and health education. She has written two other books: *Preacher's Daughter, Preacher's Kids, Church Kids: the phenomenon of growing up crazy in the Apostolic Pentecostal Church*, and *My First Period*. She holds a Bachelors in Computer Science, Masters in Secondary and Health Education, and a Doctorate in Curriculum and Instruction, from the University of North Texas. She is the adoptive-guardian mother of two daughters and one son.

Glen Etta Williams

Glen Etta Williams is the oldest sister of Jennifer Casandra Williams Herring. She and Jennifer were both reared in Baptist, then Pentecostal churches growing up, with the same father who was the Pastor of the Pentecostal church. Glen Etta attended schools in Fort Lauderdale and Pompano Beach, Florida. After graduation from high school, she entered a Nursing program for a short time, and then was one of the first of African American women hired as telephone operator at Southern Bell in Florida. She transferred to Dallas, Texas to Southwestern Bell, where she later retired. She attended a design school in Dallas, eventually opening her own business as a designer-seamstress. She is currently retired, living in Gainesville, Florida.

www.ingramcontent.com/pod-product-compliance
Lightning Source LLC
Chambersburg PA
CBHW042333150426
43194CB00001B/47